Higher Education for National Development: One Model for Technical Assistance

Kenneth W. Thompson

FOREWORD

It is a pleasure to share with others a paper written for a conference that is both readable and important. Such a paper was prepared by Kenneth Thompson of The Rockefeller Foundation for the conference on "Education and Development Reconsidered," held at the Villa Serbelloni in May 1972 and sponsored by both The Rockefeller and Ford Foundations.

This paper is important because it describes with care and precision how a program for university development overseas must be designed with precision and care. The Rockefeller Foundation has, of course, a reputation for designing custom-made programs made possible by an appropriate admixture of office wisdom, detachment, and adequate endowment.

Kenneth Thompson's document serves to remind us what a high-quality overseas development project is really like, how it is run, and how it can be honestly assessed. The International Council for Educational Development is pleased to make this report available to its special audience around the world.

James A. Perkins

Copyright ©by International Council for Educational Development
Library of Congress Catalog No. 72-93267
Printed in U.S.A. November 1972

Beginning in the early 1960s, The Rockefeller Foundation undertook to provide technical assistance for overall university development to a few selected institutions in developing countries. The program had a definable *rationale*, involved institutions selected in accordance with explicit *criteria*, proceeded according to a design or *plan* through various stages of development and undertook to assist the building of institutional *capacity* for grappling with problems of national development. These four topics provide a focus for the description of this particular approach to University Development which follows.

Rationale
Institution-building is at the heart of the Foundation's tradition. Its beginnings go back to the birth of two score schools of public health in the 1920s and 1930s, to area-studies centers in the 1950s, and to international institutes of agriculture in the 1960s. The rationale of the University Development Program (UDP) was rooted in this tradition plus the belief that, for the LDCs, the missing factor was educated people or trained leadership. Needed were not only the doctors, engineers, agronomists, and economists who would chart the nation's course but those who could multiply themselves by training men to fill such posts. The single most important factor separating the successes of the Marshall Plan from the problems of Point Four was the human and organizational infrastructure. From Point Four to the present, assistance to the developing countries has oftentimes been held in suspense when local counterpart requirements could not be met whether in trained manpower or effective institutions. The remedy lies not with outsiders; to meet these human deficits, indigenous institutions are needed to prepare the missing leaders.

A second part of the rationale underlying institution-building is that a concentrated attack on a single urgent problem, while necessary, is insufficient. Often the only thing worse than failure may be success. It is imperative to identify pressing human needs, but no less imperative to grasp their interrelationships. The earlier triumphs of public health in reducing mortality have had some part in ushering in the population explosion. The "green revolution" of our time will ultimately prove successful only if its relationship with employment, internal migration, and political structures is recognized and dealt with.

Developing universities provide a framework within which problems of this order can be considered as part of an integrated effort. One of the dividends of a technical assistance staff working together on an across-the-board basis within an institutional framework is the possibility of interdisciplinary cooperation. For decades, Rockefeller Foundation leadership had talked about a genuine multidisciplinary approach to local development problems for a well-defined and delineated geographical area. The one attempt which had been made was in the late 1940s, in Crete. It was at best a partial success but valuable lessons were learned. The Foundation's professional staff had a long tradition of operating abroad but characteristically in the more or less isolated medical or agricultural sectors. University Development has brought staff and resources together to join in the task of building educational institutions. A university can be a prime mover in the transition from traditional to modern ways of life but this requires many different kinds of trained people. It must build professional competence in key disciplines and furnish a scientific and scholarly base for relevant problem-solving. The provision of human and material capital, of people and things, is directed toward this purpose.

Criteria of selection
Once The Rockefeller Foundation decided in the 1950s to shift program emphasis from Europe and the United States to the developing countries, it was faced with critical problems of choice. It had to measure unlimited human need against severely limited resources. There was concern that, even with income being augmented through expenditure of capital, the comparatively small sums available could readily be frittered away, leaving hardly a trace over the vast reaches of Asia and Africa. At an earlier point, scatteration had prevailed: in a single year, grants or study awards were made to approximately 50 separate institutions in Latin America alone. What was the effect? Institutionally, it was minimal; for the individual returning from study, he was bereft of a post and driven into the general labor market.

This led the trustees and officers to evoke once again the principle of concentration. In the same way that an earlier decision had been made to work with one Ministry of Health or Ministry of Agriculture in a chosen country, it was decided to work with one university. The choice of the right university was a difficult one. The Foundation was determined to work only with institutions that had the potential of serving national or regional needs. As the program unfolded, a set of criteria evolved for the selection of UDP centers. The first was the existence of a genuine request for help formally and informally communicated. Review teams comprised of representatives of all sectors of program at the Foundation visited each prospective center to determine whether help was desired and to what extent conditions for indigenous growth in a given discipline were present. They "put down the scientists' rod" to test the depth and potential of resources in fields in which the Foundation could be helpful. They looked for determination to move ahead, for academic and administrative leadership committed to change, and for the prospect of increasing support from other sources.

In the same way that not every nation has made the hard decisions prerequisite to benefiting from foreign assistance, not every institution has prepared itself for genuine organic growth. It may have failed to come forward with a practical design for upgrading its faculty, neglected research opportunities, overlooked salary problems, or forgotten about community support. It may have lacked a nucleus of devoted and responsible leaders willing and able to foster institutional growth, if necessary at the expense of their own professional advancement and prestige. There are certain matters that institutions, no less than individuals or nations, cannot leave to chance. What is to be their role in a wider geographic region? How are they to weigh numerical growth against the pursuit of excellence? How much or how little should they undertake in a specific field? Is their mission to train the teachers, public servants, engineers, and doctors to serve the nation and other social and educational institutions? Or is their role conceived in more parochial, if worthy, terms of building a civic culture for their immediate constituents? Finally, has the leadership made a fresh and self-critical review of strengths and weaknesses and laid down the broad guidelines for responding to institutional needs? Recognizing that its resources are always more restricted than its needs, how far has it gone in establishing priorities for determining points of emphasis next year, three, or five years hence?

Partners in institution-building, who can at best assist only a few institutions, cannot escape the obligation to assess the many factors essential to growth. Perhaps what is needed is an institutional equivalent of the pilot's check list before clearing the aircraft for flight. But in the end, when the many factors essential to growth have been considered, partners must consider the institution as a whole. For whether the aim is developing a university or building a strong and vital research institute, the organization is somehow more than the sum of its parts. Those who assess in order to help must acquire the knack of measuring the potential and strength of institutions in the process of evolving. Universities in some parts of the world are little more than loose collections of faculties. If it is the university that invites development, this fact may lead to their exclusion, or it may require a new approach to institution-building. If outside donor organizations concentrate their resources at a few developing institutions, the corollary of their assistance is single-minded concentration by indigenous leadership on the central problems of institution-building.

Perhaps the most crucial criterion is the estimate those who assist must make of the prospects of partnership. Full and frank exchange of ideas is the result, not the forerunner, of mutual commitment. Yet intimate, unguarded, and self-critical discussion is vital if assistance is to make a difference. To mold a partnership in institution-building is to build a framework within which consultation goes on and mutually acceptable, far-reaching decisions are made. By contrast, casual involvement in institutional development results in hit-or-miss direction of those actions that shape the future. Whether the subject is selection of a fellow or reworking the syllabus or planning a new curriculum, the partners are engaged in what is ultimately the institution's most serious business. Whether they succeed or fail depends on whether these topics are considered casually en route to the airport or through the solemn and deliberate processes of ongoing institutional life.

Foundation's Plan
If the Foundation could call on universities to have a plan, it was obligated to have one too. The great issue was whether its staff could match up resources and capacities with urgent needs at selected institutions. Objectives had to be formulated in terms of definable tasks. It was vital that there be a timetable; the plan required a beginning, a middle, and an end. In operational language, the

Foundation had "to get in and get out." In 1961, the Foundation's President, J. George Harrar, in presenting the program, spoke of a possible 12–15 year effort which might cost up to $100 million. The Trustees accepted the proposal without blinking. In fact, expenditures over the first eight years totaled about $40 million.

Broadly speaking, the plan envisaged at least four distinct phases, varying as between the several UDP models described below. Phase I involves the giving of assistance in speeding the transition from a colonial to a national university. Toward this end, the Foundation may make available, on long-term assignments, a few members of its professional staff. The prior question involves identifying and defining discrete and manageable areas of assistance. This need is an outgrowth of the essential nature of technical assistance. Outside help, even public and international agency help, is inevitably marginal help. (At the peak of the Marshall Plan, the flow of aid never exceeded 4 percent of Europe's capital needs.) Private foundations particularly must come to a judicious determination of the focus of their aid. Policies follow questions that go to the heart of cooperative efforts. What are the recipient country's most urgent and pressing needs and what is it doing about them? What is it doing for itself and what does it seek from others? Viewed realistically, what capacity does the donor agency possess, or can it acquire, for assistance in those areas where it can make a genuine difference? Whether the choice is agriculture or virus research or improving an economics faculty, there are dividends in defining and identifying areas of need and matching them against available outside resources.

In Thailand, The Rockefeller Foundation has concentrated its efforts in university development on the strengthening of three basic disciplines: medical and basic sciences, agriculture, and economics. Within its operating agricultural programs, the emphasis has been on research and training programs directed toward strengthening various countries' ability to produce certain basic food crops, such as corn, wheat, sorghum, potatoes, and rice. Crops were chosen because they were crucial for specific economies—corn and wheat in Mexico, rice and sorghum in Asia. The goal has been improved varieties and techniques, not across the entire agricultural spectrum, but in areas where need and capacity could be joined. Again, in the Foundation's university development efforts, its focus has been on disciplines ready and able to use assistance for which the sources of intellectual cooperation were in sight.

Career Service

Once the major thrust has been determined, the selection of visitors and professionals skilled in the complexities of institution-building follows. Here a career service of men engaged in assistance to developing institutions is essential. The Gardner Report (1) proposed an AID career service backstopped by a cadre of Agency for International Development (AID) reservists. Experiences that hark back to the International Health Division of The Rockefeller Foundation point the way to the maintenance of professional competence for international service. If Henry Wriston is right when he states that first-class problems attract first-class minds, the rallying of qualified personnel should not be impossible. The Rockefeller Foundation, in its University Development Program, has been encouraged by the interest of first-rate scholars in serving abroad as visiting professors, heads of departments or research institutes, and even as deans. Some have been recruited as regular Foundation staff, others as temporary personnel, and others as scholars on leave from their own universities. A career service for university development must be flexible enough to provide for commitments ranging across a sliding scale of interest. Some will be engaged more or less permanently, others for a year or two. It is obvious that any plan for a career service that would attract the best minds must allow for both service and research—the continuation of a scholar's most deeply cherished interests. Essential will be the presence, in any organized effort at a university development center, of at least a few top-flight leaders devoting themselves full time to academic administration and teaching. Their presence at the heart of the development enterprise leaves room for researchers who teach by carrying forward their inquiries.

In the end, the fate of American education abroad is dependent on responsible and well-qualified people engaged in tasks for which there is recognized need. Sometimes this involves doing well what a scholar is required to do in any educational setting. At other times the adaptation must be more drastic. Perhaps the success of the American educational effort is greatest when the approach is indirect and oblique. American

---

1. John W. Gardner, *AID and the Universities*, New York: Education and World Affairs, 1964.

agronomists, economists, or virologists probably contribute most when they labor as scientists and scholars drawing on the full range of knowledge which they can appropriate not because they are Americans, but because of professional competence. If this is the test of American education, it is more likely to be realized within the framework of an organized, concentrated, career-oriented approach to institution-building abroad.

The corollary of the concept of a career service is the need to build supplementary structures and arrangements for strengthening institutions abroad. The ICA/AID* philosophy of sister university relationships was a creative invention for institution-building, but suffered in its implementation. It was sometimes plagued by misunderstandings, mediocrity, and inflexibility, but the heart of the idea was sound. There are by-products of university-to-university cooperation that serve both institutions and their personnel.

The Rockefeller Foundation, in this spirit, has made approximately 25 university grants to institutions in Great Britain, France, Canada, Switzerland, and the United States, patterned after the arrangements described in the Gardner Report—but with a difference. First, the universities concerned extend assistance to developing institutions through visiting professors and cooperating junior colleagues in specific disciplines. For example, the Yale Growth Center, the Williams College Institute of Economic Development, and Northwestern University give help in Economics. Princeton, Notre Dame, Cornell, Duke, Michigan, Wisconsin, and Minnesota Universities send visitors in the Social Sciences, as do Toronto, Sussex, and McGill Universities. Second, the developing universities themselves play a determining role in the selection of cooperating Western universities and the choice of individual professors. Third, a schedule is worked out of visitors for successive academic years so that both the developing and developed universities can plan for the years ahead. Fourth, the professionals concerned, including career service personnel at the developing universities, play an active role, not only in selecting visiting professors but defining their role and working out the most meaningful assignments before they arrive. It would be impossible to exaggerate the pivotal role of the senior foundation representative in planning,

---

* ICA (International Cooperation Administration) was the predecessor agency to AID, responsible for administering foreign aid.

consulting, and paving the way for the visitors and assuring they have a serious piece of work to do without wasted time and effort. Fifth, the watchword is flexibility. A particular Western university, principally engaged in strengthening university X, is not precluded from assisting university Y. Equally, university X can receive help from more than one source, if appropriate. Sixth, the role of visitors is part of a total university development plan and their contributions are made to mesh with the overall design.

Phases I—IV
The machinery for assisting developing universities is of course less important than its purpose. Once an institution has entered into a cooperative program with the Foundation, the first step for those who come to help is to make themselves expendable. Through fellowships and scholarships—for study both locally and abroad—the training of national educational leaders is facilitated; counterpart relationships between visitors and emerging national leaders are integral to the process. The Foundation's 54-year fellowship program, under which over 10,000 fellowships have been awarded, has proven an indispensable factor in this aspect of the University Development Program. (See Table A.) As scholars return, key academic departments come under local leadership and there is a magic moment of change to which visitors must be sensitive and alert. There is a time for visitors to leave or move to the backgound—but when is it? Is it when three Ph.D's have returned to a department, when one is serving as departmental chairman, or when two-thirds of the departments are under local leadership? (2)

The tests for the ending of Phase I are at best rough and ready and the developmental phase, even for disciplines with initially favorable prospects, may vary from a period of five to ten years. But at some point, cooperating institutions must assume that the first chapter is complete. It is time to change the form and substance of cooperation. Phase II signals the emergence of national leadership. However tempting it may be to protest that the transfer of responsibility is premature, the issue at this point is not negotiable. No one should expect that the new leadership will be carbon copies of the old. The type of person sent

---

2. It is obvious that departments within the same university may be in different phases of development at the same point in time.

TABLE A

Study Awards 1963–1971

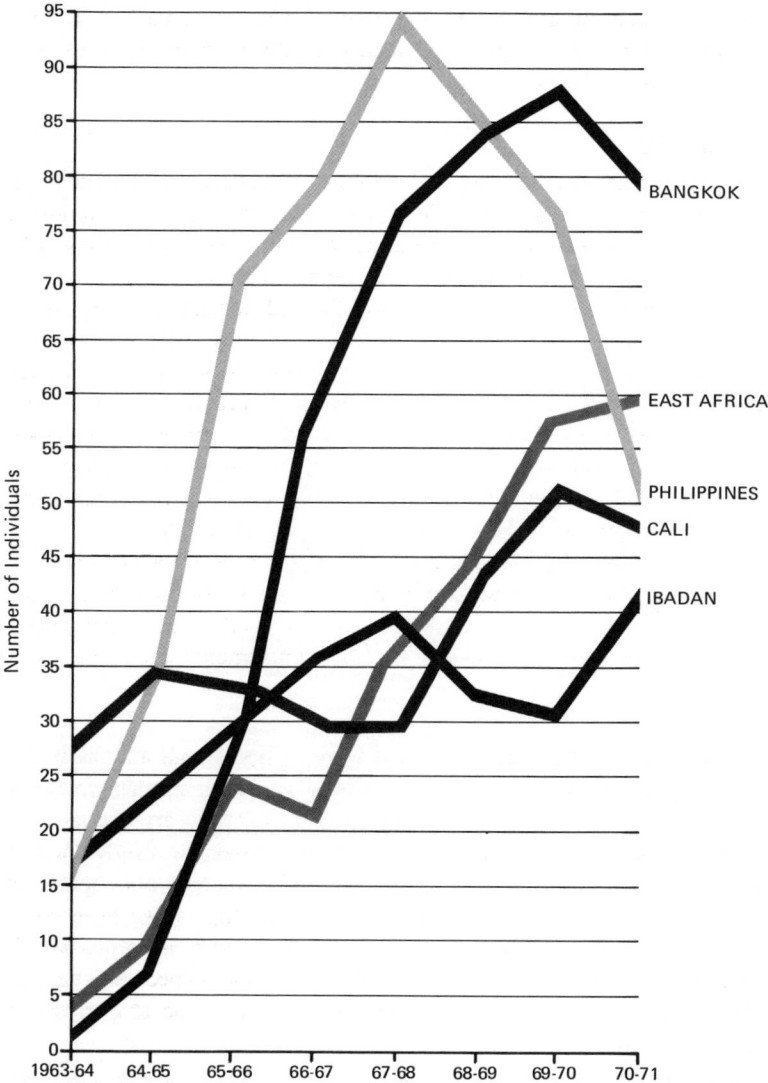

abroad to assist in Phase II should be more an advisor than an institution-builder, patient and responsive rather than aggressive, and willing to work through others while remaining in the background. His aim should be less to initiate, more to plant ideas in the minds of others. If Phase I requires a critical mass of outside institution-builders, Phase II calls for a very few, low-profile advisors. The time required for Phase II may be anywhere from one to three years.

Phase III is a period of consolidation, of putting new capacities and institutions to work. It involves planning for graduate programs, serving the community, and turning emergent human resources toward the solution of national and regional problems. Phase III is a period of reaping the harvest of earlier developmental efforts. The application of trained intelligence to problem-solving is for the first time fully possible. Not by accident, each of the International Agriculture Institutes is located next to a university development center. Equally, an attack on unemployment problems profits from economics, engineering, and agricultural resources in university centers.

Phase IV is a time for giving back by those who have received. It involves first-generation university development centers helping second-generation centers. Thus, leadership in the newest UDP center at the University of Bahia is being provided by men such as Gabriel Velazquez of Universidad del Valle, at the University of Zaïre by leaders from the University of East Africa, or by Philippine economists such as Dr. Jose Encarnacion teaching and directing research in Thailand and Indonesia.

To be effective a plan must be flexible, taking its cue from the strengths and weaknesses within each institution and adapting its timetable to changing needs. Because institutions differ, forms of assistance vary. The university centers which have been assisted fall into at least four broad categories or models (the Foundation over the past decade has given some form of assistance to approximately 10 institutions or complexes of universities but major support has been concentrated in five centers *).

---

* The UDP centers are: *Colombia:* Universidad del Valle; *East Africa:* University of East Africa (since July 1, 1970–Makerere University, Kampala; The University of Dar es Salaam, University of Nairobi); *Nigeria*: University of Ibadan; *Philippines*: University of the Philippines; *Thailand*: Kasetsart University, Mahidol University, Thammasat University.

Universidad del Valle

Model I is university development in which the Foundation has been virtually a co-equal partner over a sustained period, sharing a major part of costs and manpower needs. The Universidad del Valle is a provincial university in Cali, Colombia, with a student body of 5,000 and a new concept of a university for a developing country. Its goal has been to keep the university close to the community addressing itself to urgent social needs. It has been a leader in medical education for all of Latin America, directing the interests of students toward rural peoples through mandatory clinical residency in the Candelaria Rural Health Center, and teaching preventive medicine, child care and family planning. In the early 1960s, the Medical School, which had enjoyed assistance throughout the 1950s, towered over the rest of the University, but a concerted effort was made to help raise the level of Engineering, Economics and Agricultural Economics, University Administration, the Humanities and the Basic Sciences. The proportion of Foundation support to the total university budget is indicated in Table I.

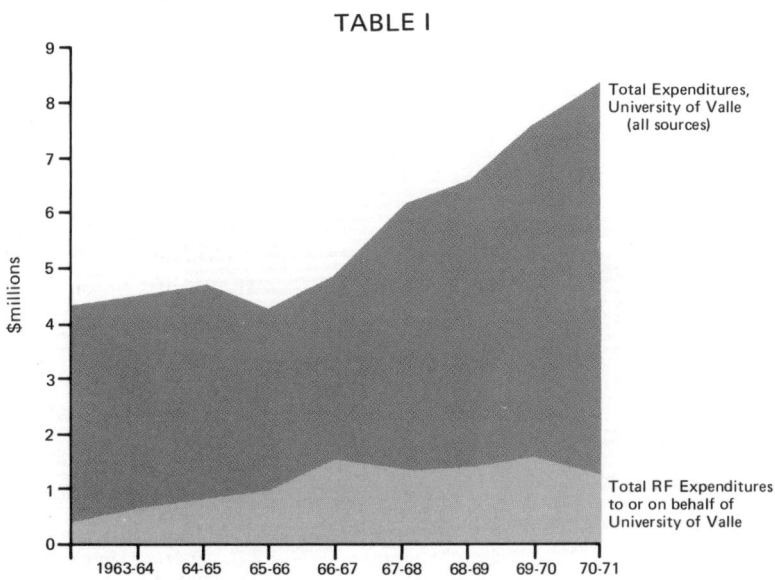

TABLE I

TABLE II

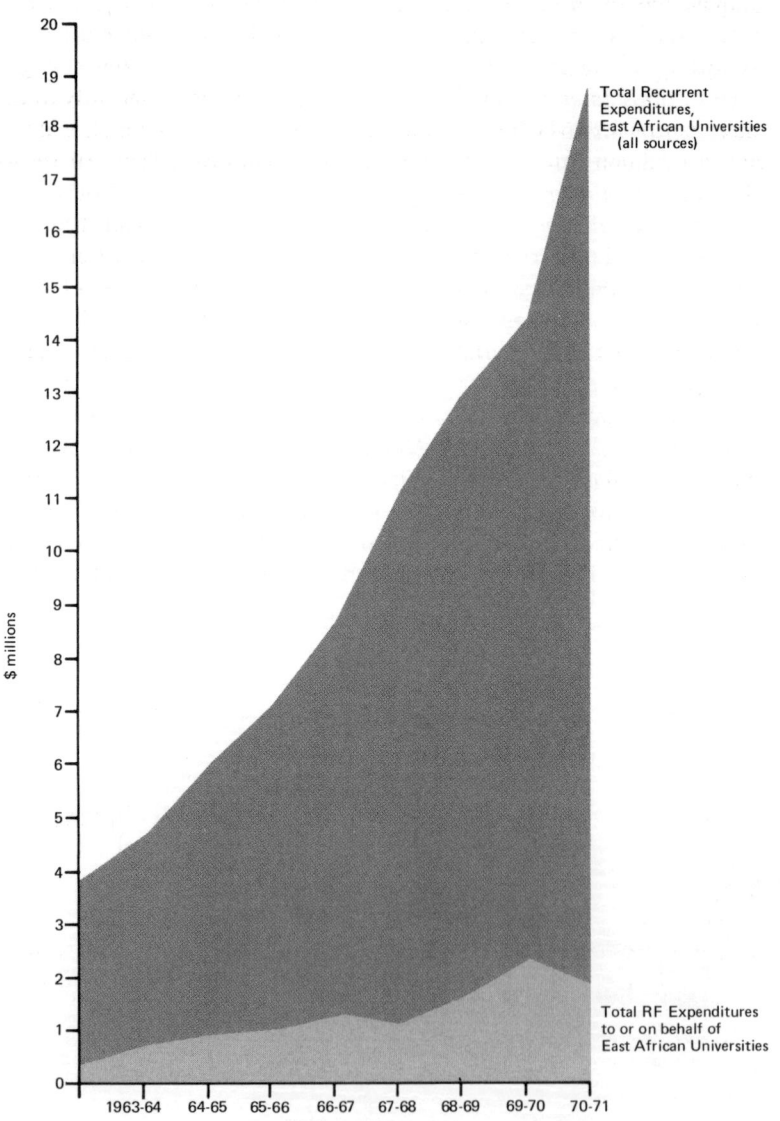

East Africa

Model II finds the Foundation—as in East Africa—playing the role of catalytic agent, helping to initiate change or, in Raymond Fosdick's graphic phrase, providing the "extra engine put on to help . . . over a stiff grade." As indicated in Table II, the Foundation's contribution has always been minor, first to the three independent national colleges, then to the federated University of East Africa, and most recently to the three national universities bound together by numerous functional ties and a common Inter-University Committee. However, Table III shows that 66 percent of all East African faculty have been Rockefeller Foundation scholars or holders of Special Lectureships established with Rockefeller Foundation funding for returning national scholars for whom an established post was not yet available. If the sample is limited to East Africans who are full professors and deans, 80 percent have had assistance. The Agricultural Faculty at Makerere College in Uganda reoriented its curriculum with greater emphasis on crop production during the leadership of Dean John Nickel, Rockefeller Foundation staff member. The Institute of Development Studies in Nairobi reached maturity in the years of Dr. James S. Coleman's directorship. For a far-flung multinational university in these countries, help at crucial points can affect the entire university even though the total resources provided from outside may be small relative to the overall educational budget.

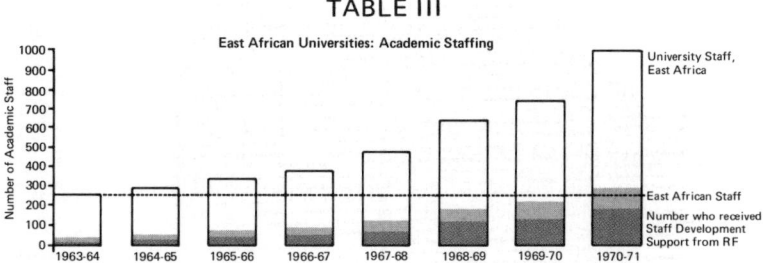

TABLE III

East African Universities: Academic Staffing

University of the Philippines
Model III involves help to more fully developed universities to complete or round out institutional development, or some aspect of that development. At the University of the Philippines, the application of this approach is illustrated in a dual sense. When General Carlos P. Romulo became President in 1963, he declared he would seek help for fields other than Agriculture, Engineering, and Medicine, which had been strengthened through outside assistance over the years. Unless other areas including the Social Sciences and Humanities could be developed, Romulo was convinced the University would not be worthy of the name. At the same time the University pressed ahead to bring the Graduate Program in Economics to the Ph.D. level and to establish the Agriculture Faculty as a regional center for Graduate Studies. In both instances, the Foundation provided supplementary fellowship funds and visiting professors to fill gaps until local faculty returned from study abroad.

Bangkok
Model IV involves help to strong points in a complex of universities within a city or region or to independent but cooperating universities. Institution-building in Agriculture, the Biomedical Sciences and Economics has been fostered in three separate universities: Kasetsart, Mahidol, and Thammasat respectively, in Bangkok, Thailand; the strategy has been one of building on existing strength at the three centers. (Table IV traces the Mahidol program.) The goal for each has been the building of institutional strength capable of serving a wider geographical region (nine young Indonesian scientists are currently engaged in Ph.D. study at Mahidol University). While ideally university development should go on within the walls of a single institution, practically differing forms of institutional cooperation are possible with aggregate effects similar to the strengthening of one university. Once again, imagination and flexibility are of the essence. Table V depicts the total efforts of the Foundation in UDP and traces the phases of help at each institution.

Universities and National Development
The two lessons of greatest moment that derive from a decade's experience with The Rockefeller Foundation's UDP model are: (1) the need for scientists and educators working abroad to operate within a

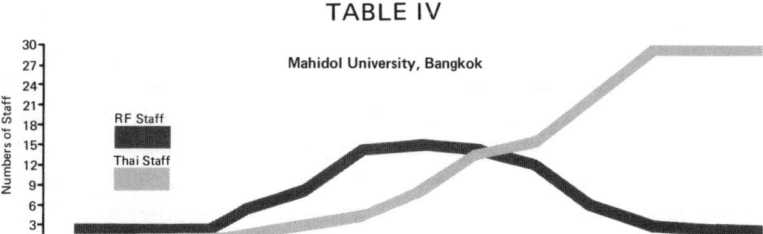

TABLE IV

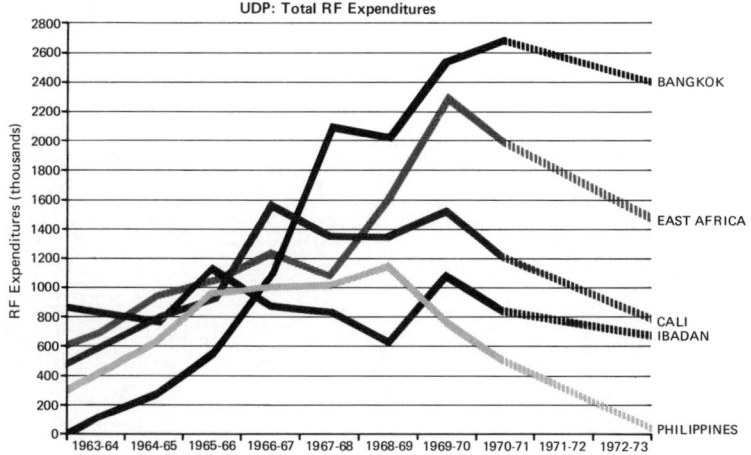

TABLE V

framework reflecting the interrelatedness of human problems and knowledge; and (2) the need for continuity within a broad strategy or design having definable stages of development and looking toward points of completion.

With regard to the first, the very successes of foreign assistance can create new challenges and problems, some more exacting and perplexing than the failures. The work of development too often has been a "catch-up" operation. It is probably unfair to say that the success of the International Health Division created the population explosion-but surely it was a contributing factor. Improved health, lower mortality rates, and longer lifespans thereby add to a nation's problems. We see now some of the hazards in pursuing health or agricultural programs in isolation. The unique opportunity that university development presents is that advances on one front can be coordinated with determined and concentrated efforts along other fronts. Programs in improved health delivery systems can go on simultaneously with population control. Efforts to increase food production can be accompanied by inquiries into the economic and social consequences of the "green revolution." Instead of "catching up," the developing countries can be assisted in preparing for the problems that lie ahead three, five or ten years down the road.

On the second lesson—the need for continuity within a broad design—there is a striking difference between the approach of the International Health Division or the cooperative agricultural programs and many undertakings in international cooperation. It is sometimes noted that foreign assistance often involves the struggle to meet twenty-year needs with a three-year program, two-year personnel, and one-year appropriations. By contrast, The Rockefeller Foundation's Mexican Agricultural Program was inaugurated in 1943. It has evolved from a limited exploratory effort, through a national program carefully housed in the Office of Special Studies within the Ministry of Agriculture, to the current International Maize and Wheat Improvement Center. Almost 30 years later, a handful of the original team of Rockefeller Foundation agricultural scientists continue to serve as participant advisors in a fully Mexican international agricultural program, aiming to share with others the accumulated knowledge developed over the past three decades.

There is a time to give assistance and a time to withhold it or bring it to an end. The University of the Philippines, under the vital and dynamic leadership of General Carlos P. Romulo, reached the stage, particularly in the Arts and Sciences, where strategically placed assistance could enable it to move to a new level of excellence. How shortsighted it would have been for agencies that had faithfully provided fellowship help in other periods in its history to have terminated aid at that point. Now, with the growing nationalization of the university the possibilities and need for aid become more restricted and more sharply defined. But continuity of effort is essential if enduring institutions are to be developed.

The ultimate goal of institution-building is of course national development—to widen the range of choice open to the general population, improve the quality of life, and serve the most urgent needs of the people. As nations undertake this complex and many-sided task, they must rely to a large degree upon the strengths and involvement of their universities, with their necessary concentrations of talent. The universities, to be effectively involved, must understand the nation's needs and how best to meet them; this requires that universities participate with other agencies in the planning and execution of national programs. In this way the university faculty and students can contribute to national progress as they teach and learn. Course offerings should become increasingly relevant, as new information related to national need is developed. University graduates should be much better equipped with both the knowledge and skills required for participation in accelerated national development. Faculty must increasingly teach from a basis of understanding derived both from a study of efforts of others (past and present) and from experience gained through involvement in meeting real needs of the region and people served by the university. Nor should the study of the humanities and social values be ignored for these are determinants of the ways knowledge and skills will be used.

As universities demonstrate their usefulness not only as centers of scholarly effort but as institutions capable of joining scholarship with effective action, appreciation of them and support for them can be expected to follow.

As Dr. Sterling Wortman, speaking of agriculture, said at Bellagio, Italy:

What, then, should be the nature of the activities of an agricultural college, and how should its success be measured? It would seem that at least two criteria would be useful: (a) the student's proficiency in the use of the knowledge and understanding gained through his university experience; and (b) the impact of the college's research program on the nation's economic development.

Each central agricultural college should have on its staff a number of specialists who, through years of dedicated experience, have emerged as authorities in their fields. At a good college in the tropics, one should expect to find authorities on each crop or animal species of major importance or potential importance in the region served. One should also find specialists on the major animal and plant diseases and on major insect problems, as well as specialists in economics, agricultural engineering, and other fields.

Each crop or animal specialist should be providing leadership for important components of the overall research program for the area served, whether this be a province, a region, or a nation. His program should be closely integrated with those of the action agencies of the ministry of agriculture, and with extension agencies that may be administered separately. There must be a minimum of administrative barriers between the central experiment station and the farmer. If leadership of major research activities has been vested in a different research organization, then university personnel still must contribute significantly to the total effort....

The medical profession usually requires that a candidate for the M.D. degree spend a substantial period of time as an intern under the guidance of qualified professionals. Agricultural colleges might well require a year's internship in a dynamic research program as a prerequisite to graduation. This, however, would require crop- or animal-oriented research programs—well-equipped experiment stations with staff members working on critical problems in the region served—which in turn would require the presence of effective and continuing scientific leadership. (3)

---

3. Dr. Wortman's paper, entitled "The Technological Basis for Intensified Agriculture," was prepared for a conference sponsored by The Rockefeller Foundation at Villa Serbelloni, Bellagio, Italy, April 23–25, 1969. The paper appears in a report of that conference, "Agricultural Development: Proceedings of a Conference."

It is of course difficult to measure quantitatively the influence of universities on national economic, social, and cultural development but clearly significant inputs have been made through the UDP effort. For example, the Development Economics training program, undertaken by the School of Economics in the University of the Philippines for members of the government economic civil service, has made a difference in the quality of operation of the economic secretariat. The School of Economics' research program, with its focus on Philippine development problems, has led to significant governmental policy changes. A faculty member is currently on leave serving as chairman of the National Economic Council and has drawn heavily on his colleagues for relevant policy-oriented studies. Clearly the university is making a difference.

The emphasis on a better understanding of African history, under the leadership of a succession of outstanding Nigerian historians at the University of Ibadan, is developing a better understanding of Nigeria's history and cultural heritage—a most important element in nation-building but one with a delayed impact. A number of Ibadan faculty members have served on a wide variety of state and federal government panels and study commissions, including very substantial participation in creating the last Nigerian development plan. The Bureau of Resource Assessment and Land Use Planning of the University of Dar es Salaam has geared its total research efforts to priority needs as outlined in the Tanzanian development plan, with a significant impact in the rural areas.

In Kenya, the Institute for Development Studies in the University of Nairobi was created as a multidisciplinary organization in response to a strongly felt need for organized, full-time research on urgent social and economic problems of development. It is concerned with the basic, long-term development problems as well as more immediately pressing policy issues. Current research projects reflect the national needs with a focus on rural development, urban and industrial development, employment, and education. At present, the Institute is deeply involved as a partner in the ILO employment studies in Kenya.

The Vice-Chancellor of the University of Nairobi, Dr. J. N. Karanja, who was the first East African scholar to be appointed to the post of special lecturer with Rockefeller Foundation support, has written:

As a major national institution the University of Nairobi has a duty, an opportunity and a determination to contribute significantly to all aspects of Kenya's national development. In co-operation with our Government, with other departments and institutes of the University, and with all other agencies concerned with development—national, regional and international—the Institute for Development Studies is responsible for initiating, co-ordinating and directing its own programme of applied and interdisciplinary research on high-priority social and economic problems of development of Kenya in particular and of Eastern Africa in general. This broad mandate includes the provision of research opportunities, facilities and professional guidance for the study of problems of development to a rapidly expanding number of Kenyans interested in academic or other careers in the service of the nation; the accelerated Africanisation of university teaching and other instructional materials based on research on the development problems of our own society; and the maintenance of a centre of intellectual stimulus and productivity with which visiting scholars from all over the world can be associated and to which they can make their own contribution to human knowledge as well as to the development of our nation. (4)

The participation of the Biomedical Sciences in the University Development program can range from the minimal, as in East Africa, to a maximum effort, as in Bangkok. In each instance, two factors must be taken into consideration: first, the university's view of its own needs in medical education; and, second, the actual needs of the communities as estimated by outside evaluators. Many medical faculties will express a desire for an organ transplant team, whereas the simplest community evaluation will indicate that their primary need is in the less glamorous control of infectious diseases.

From these experiences, the most significant development has been in the realm of community health education. The program at Candelaria has recently received international recognition, and US-AID requested an application to expand this work to include a large urban segment as well as the rural communities already involved. The program at Bay in the Philippines represents a success that continues under government sponsorship even after the withdrawal of all Rockefeller Foundation

---

4. Institute for Development Studies, University of Nairobi, Research and Publications, January 1972. Foreword, p. 1.

personnel. The program in Bangkok, while newer, has all the earmarks of being an equal success. Each of these has served as a demonstration model in immediate health problem-solving. Thus, physicians from Central and South America are sent on fellowships to study the program at Candelaria and, hopefully, to return and implement similar ventures in their own countries. The physicians involved in the community health teaching in Bangkok have been invited to present two different training sessions in different universities in Malaysia. These programs contain elements of family planning and perinatal care with whatever additional features the health of the community demands (nutrition, control of infectious diseases, etc.).

In many ways, these community health programs, which represent but a fraction of the Biomedical Science participation in University Development programs, represent one of the best contributions that University Development can make. They are action programs and tend to refocus the curriculum and the students' thinking toward the local health needs rather than toward the emulation of the super-specialized medicine of the developed countries.

Countless other examples could be given of the ways in which universities—their staff and students—are responding to the economic, social and cultural developmental needs in the various countries. The pace is uneven, and impatient observers may say the responses are too slow and not on a large enough scale. However, as one views the changes which have occurred over the past decade, the transformation has been deep and profound. Many universities are developing into institutions capable of adapting existing knowledge and creating new knowledge and technologies more appropriate to the social and economic resources of the less developed countries. An impressive impact has been made but clearly a great challenge remains.

Ten years of experimenting with university development make it clear that national development is no simple one-dimensional process. It is more than industrial growth, increased food production, or preparing economists or engineers. The values by which men live, the social structures within which they make choices, and the political systems they espouse may be as crucial as material advances. A university development approach helps donors and recipients to recognize the multiple dimensions of national development and make some modest contribution wherever possible.

International Council For Educational Development

The International Council for Educational Development (ICED) is an international non-profit association of persons with a common concern for the future of education and its role in social and economic development.

ICED's three major interests are strategies for educational development; the modernization and management of systems of higher education; and the international programs and responsibilities of higher education. In each area, ICED's purposes are to identify and analyze major educational problems shared by a number of countries, to generate policy recommendations, and to provide consultation, on request, to international and national organizations.

ICED's activities are directed by James A. Perkins, chief executive officer and chairman of an international board. Philip H. Coombs is vice chairman. The headquarters office is in New York City. ICED's European representative, Max Kohnstamm, president of the European Community Institute for University Studies, maintains an office in Brussels.

The main support for ICED to date has come from The Ford Foundation, the International Bank for Reconstruction and Development, UNICEF, and the Clark Foundation.